ARCTURUS

This edition published in 2023 by Arcturus Publishing Limited
26/27 Bickels Yard, 151–153 Bermondsey Street,
London SE1 3HA

Copyright © Arcturus Holdings Limited

Text and design: Everitt Editorial
Illustrations: Diego Funck
Editor: Violet Peto
Managing Editor: Joe Harris

ISBN: 978-1-3988-2969-5
CH010443NT
Supplier 29, Date 0523, PI 00003638

Printed in China

How to Solve Crosswords

Welcome to the book of Crosswords for Smart Kids! More than 50 puzzles are ready for you to solve, if you're up to the challenge.

To complete a crossword, solve the answer to each clue, and write your answers in the blank grid spaces (one letter per square). Start writing each answer in the square with the same number as the matching clue. Each clue has a number at the end of it—this tells you how many letters are in the answer. If the clue is in the "Across" list, write your answer left to right. If the clue is in the "Down" list, write your answer top to bottom.

You may see a semicolon (;) in some clues. The semicolon splits the clue into two parts, meaning that you have not one, but two clues to help you out!

If a clue refers to "an anagram," you'll have to do some unscrambling. An anagram takes all the letters of a word, puts them in a different order, and makes another word! For example, an anagram of "ocean" is "canoe."

Have fun!

Let It Snow

Across

3 You can do this on a snowy slope to move quickly downhill (3)

6 A delicious drink that's particularly nice on a cold day (3,9)

7 Clothing for hands, used to keep them warm (6)

9 Taller than a hill; very large landmass (8)

Down

1 Severe snowstorm with high winds (8)

2 Eye protection used when snowboarding (7)

3 A place where you can learn to **3 across** (6)

4 Ski hill; anagram of "poles" (5)

5 Frozen projectile used in a friendly winter fight (8)

8 Very top of a **9 across** (6)

Under the Sea

Across

3 This fearsome sea predator has a mouth full of razor-sharp teeth (5)

4 A soft-bodied sea animal with eight long tentacles (7)

6 A sea creature that walks sideways and has two pincers (4)

8 Someone who swims and explores underwater (5)

9 A gem found in oyster shells (5)

Down

1 A small fish that sounds as if it should be ridden by a jockey (8)

2 People wear these on their feet to help them swim (8)

5 A vessel that can travel under water (9)

7 A swimming reptile with a shell on its back (6)

Unicorn Queen

Across

2 Sparkle, especially like a star (7)

3 Unicorns need this to exist (5)

4 The number of legs on a unicorn foal (4)

5 Red, orange, yellow, green, blue, indigo, and violet (7)

6 A non-magical unicorn is called a _ _ _ _ _ (5)

Down

1 Charmingly attractive; lovely to look at (9)

2 The rear part of a unicorn's body that sticks out from the backbone (4)

4 When you need to find a unicorn, look in an enchanted _ _ _ _ _ _ (6)

6 A unicorn has one of these on the front of its head (4)

All Aboard!

Across

3 A flow of water in a river or the sea (7)

4 The leader of a ship's crew (7)

7 Light boat with sails (5)

8 Use oars to move a boat (3)

Down

1 The remains of a ship that has been destroyed or sunk (9)

2 Pretzel shape; nautical speed unit (4)

3 Goods carried by a ship, plane, train, or truck (5)

5 A sailor who steals from other ships (6)

6 Heavy object used to prevent a vessel from drifting off (6)

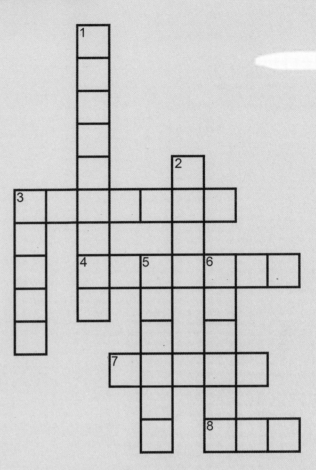

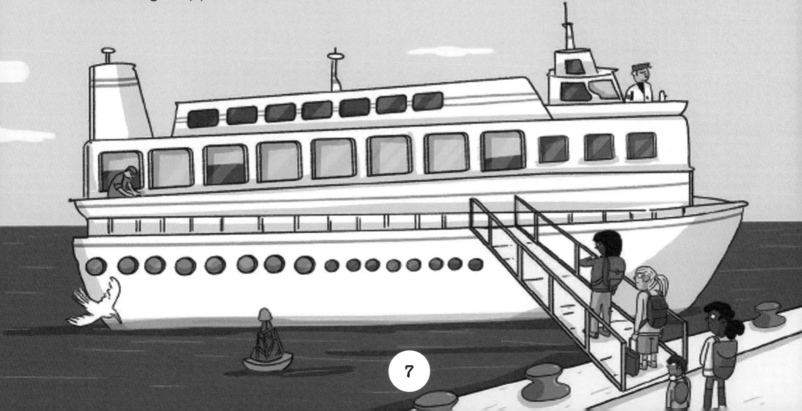

Fruit Salad

Across

3 Small soft fruit, usually dark red, with a pit in the middle (6)

5 Small, round, very dark fruit (12)

6 A large tropical fruit with yellow flesh and hard, woody skin (9)

8 A large round fruit. Varieties include cantaloupe and honeydew (5)

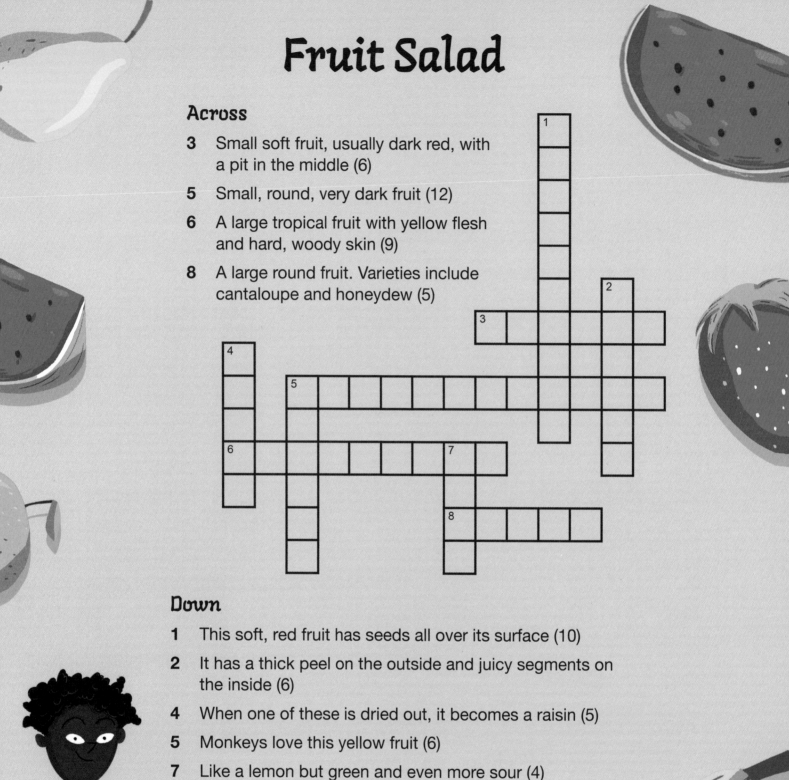

Down

1 This soft, red fruit has seeds all over its surface (10)

2 It has a thick peel on the outside and juicy segments on the inside (6)

4 When one of these is dried out, it becomes a raisin (5)

5 Monkeys love this yellow fruit (6)

7 Like a lemon but green and even more sour (4)

Old MacDonald's Farm

Across

3 Edible parts of a sunflower (5)

5 Food with a fragile shell, laid by 7 across (3)

6 Farming vehicle, often seen in fields at harvest time (7)

7 Female chickens (4)

8 Home for bees (4)

Down

1 Gather a ripened crop (7)

2 Sound made by a sheep or a goat (5)

4 Times of the year, each approximately three months long (7)

7 Group of cows (4)

Later, Alligator

Across

3 This long, slithering species of reptile has venomous fangs; spitting _ _ _ _ _ (5)

4 This giant reptile lies in wait at the water's edge, grabbing prey with its enormous snapping jaws (9)

7 Emerged from an egg (7)

8 Cast off (e.g., snake skin) (4)

Down

1 Reptile with sticky toe pads (5)

2 Water-going reptiles with bony shell and flipper-like limbs; leatherback or snapping (7)

5 This lizard hides from predators by changing its appearance to blend in with the background (9)

6 The Komodo dragon is the largest of this type of four-legged reptile (6)

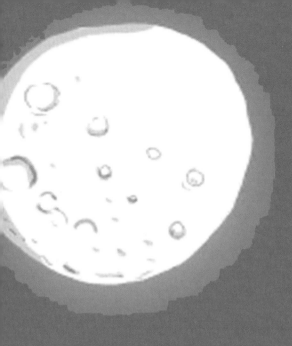
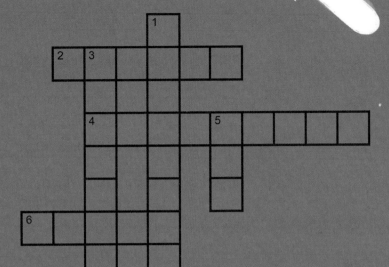

Stargazing

Across

2 A collection of star systems; any of the billions of systems, each having many stars and nebulae and dust (6)

4 Equipment used to magnify images of faraway objects; Hubble _ _ _ _ _ _ _ _ _ (9)

6 The second nearest planet to the Sun; planet visible from Earth as an early "morning star" or an "evening star" (5)

7 Planet Earth's satellite (4)

Down

1 This space visitor is visible every 76 years (7,5)

3 Person who studies space (10)

5 The closest star to Earth (3)

Fun Hobbies

Across

3 Board game with kings, queens, and pawns (5)

6 Field glasses; bird-watchers' accessories (10)

8 You might wear a tutu if you were performing this dance (6)

Down

1 What you listen to when you're dancing (5)

2 Great weather for flying a kite (5)

4 You wear this on your head to keep safe at the skate park (6)

5 A flat, curved platform that people stand on to ride through the waves (9)

7 A sticky substance that is used as an adhesive when scrapbooking (4)

Science Skills

Across

4 Area in which an animal might make its home; woodland or wetland are types of this (7)

6 A geologist studies these stones (5)

7 Branch of science relating to the study of living things (7)

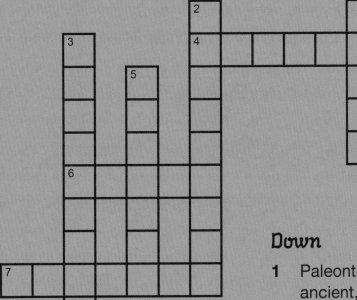

Down

1 Paleontologists study these ancient, extinct reptiles (9)

2 Science of the composition of substances (9)

3 Place for experiments; _____ coats are typically white (10)

5 Fiery mountain, e.g., Vesuvius or Etna (7)

Ice Age

Across

4 Remains of an ancient plant or animal; studied by paleontologists (6)

6 When a species dies out, it is said to be _ _ _ _ _ _ _ (7)

7 Period of time, e.g., Anthropocene, Pleistocene, Eocene (5)

Down

1 This ice-age member of the cat family had very large teeth (8)

2 Large, extinct animal related to the elephant (7)

3 Slow-moving mass of ice (7)

5 Megatherium was a type of giant ground _ _ _ _ _ (5)

Busy City

Across

4 The main city in a country, often where its government is based (7)

5 Place where you might go for treatment when sick or injured (8)

6 Collective term for vehicles; you might get stuck in this during rush hour (7)

7 Subterranean; London's subway system (11)

Down

1 These are physical places where people work, often on computers (7)

2 Trains and buses are all forms of this (6,9)

3 Shopping complex, often with a food court (4)

Birds of a Feather

Across

2 Tropical bird, often with the ability to mimic sounds (6)

5 Nocturnal hunting bird; Hogwarts messenger (3)

6 Birds often build these to house their eggs (5)

7 Common farm bird; its eggs are often eaten by humans (7)

Down

1 Plumage; down (8)

3 Common songbird, the male of which has a red chest (5)

4 Pink wading bird, often seen standing on one leg (8)

5 Large flightless African bird (7)

Bamboo-zled Bears

Across

2 The fur around a panda's eyes are this shade (5)

4 Wild pandas live in this country (5)

5 Pandas eat a lot of this plant (6)

Down

1 Any animal that eats only plants; not a carnivore (9)

2 Brown, grizzly, and panda are all types of _ _ _ _ (4)

3 Use hands and feet to ascend a tree, say (5)

4 A baby panda (3)

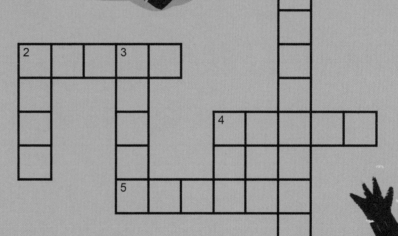

Ahoy, Me Hearties!

Across

3 Captain Jack _ _ _ _ _ _ _, a character in the *Pirates of the Caribbean* movies (7)

5 Board "walked" on a pirate ship (5)

6 Bird often seen on the shoulder of a pirate (6)

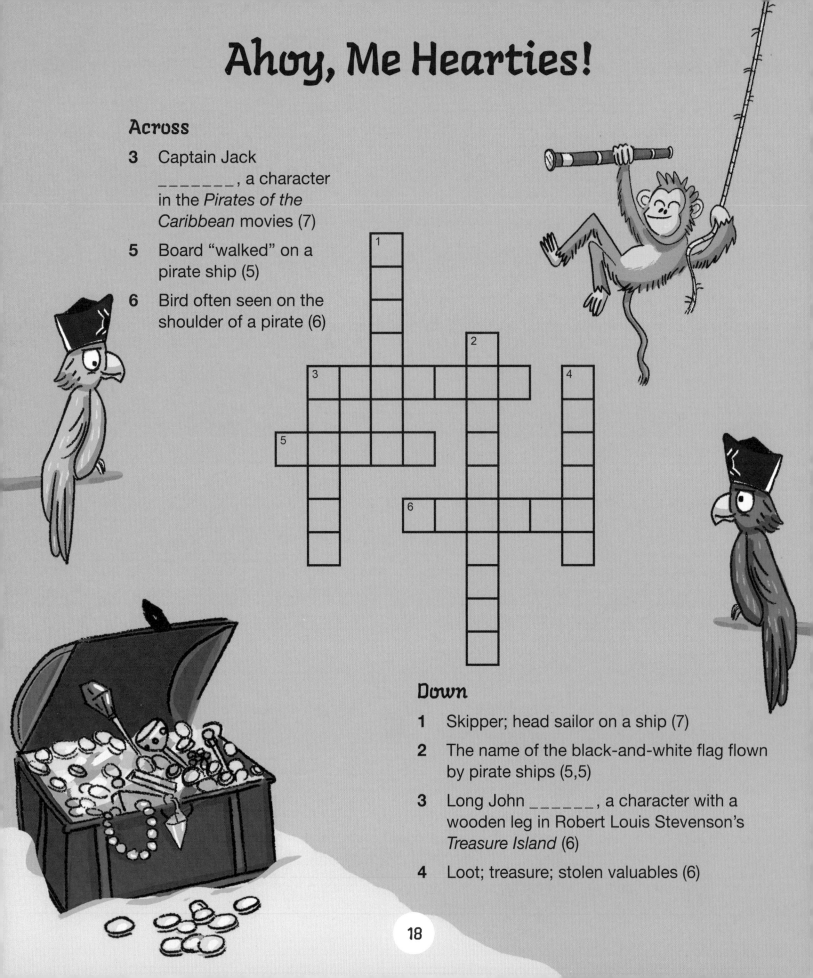

Down

1 Skipper; head sailor on a ship (7)

2 The name of the black-and-white flag flown by pirate ships (5,5)

3 Long John _ _ _ _ _ _, a character with a wooden leg in Robert Louis Stevenson's *Treasure Island* (6)

4 Loot; treasure; stolen valuables (6)

At the Gym

Across

1 Physical training or exertion; workout (8)

3 Mechanical device; running _ _ _ _ _ _ _ (7)

5 Fitness coach (7)

7 Structure filled with water, used to swim in (4)

8 Heavy things lifted to build strength; dumbbells (7)

Down

2 Jogging or sprinting (7)

4 Use these to listen to music privately (10)

6 Good physical condition (7)

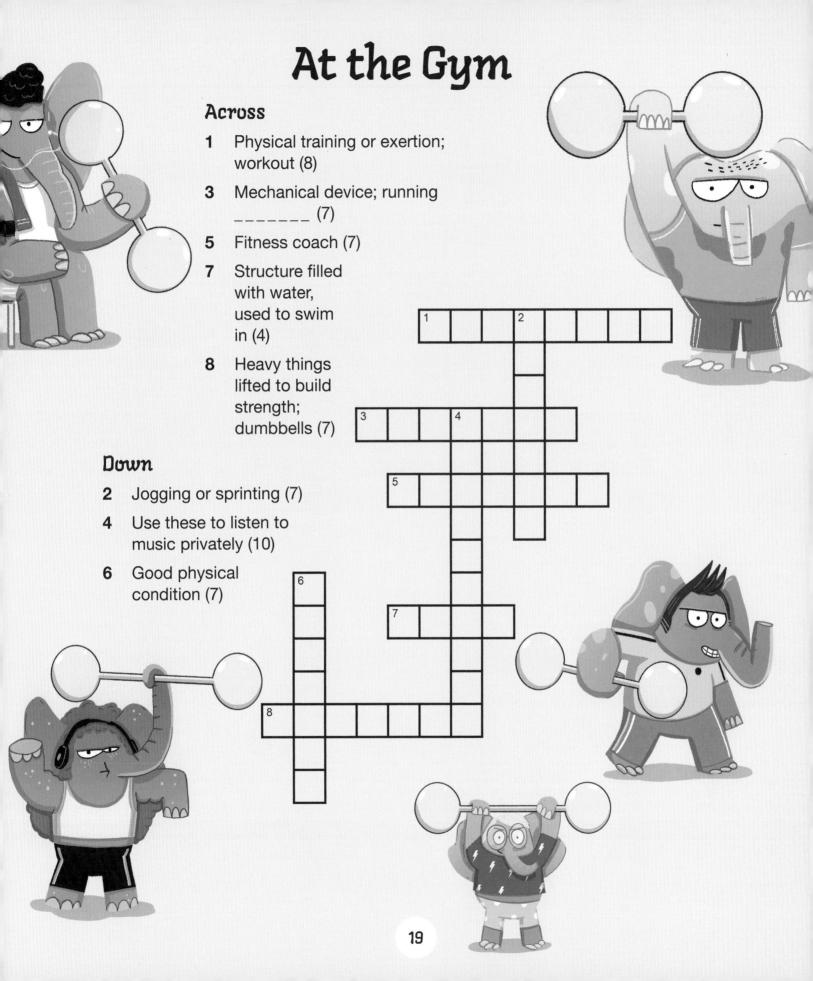

Amazing Amazon

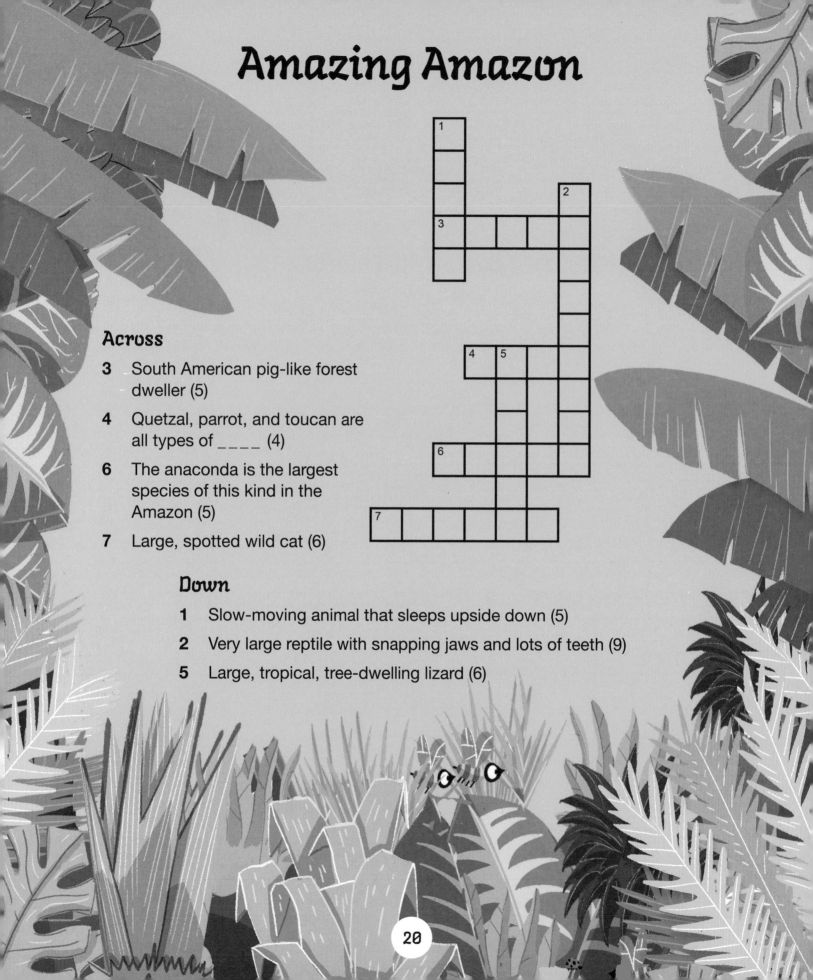

Across

3 South American pig-like forest dweller (5)

4 Quetzal, parrot, and toucan are all types of _ _ _ _ (4)

6 The anaconda is the largest species of this kind in the Amazon (5)

7 Large, spotted wild cat (6)

Down

1 Slow-moving animal that sleeps upside down (5)

2 Very large reptile with snapping jaws and lots of teeth (9)

5 Large, tropical, tree-dwelling lizard (6)

River Run

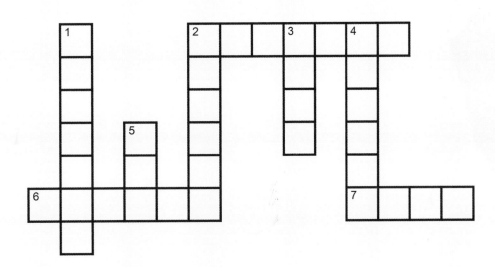

Across

2 Small water-going vessel, moved by oars (3,4)

6 Structure for crossing a river (6)

7 Egyptian river (4)

Down

1 Tidal mouth of a river (7)

2 Slight surface wave; sign of wind on water (6)

3 The ground at the side of a river (4)

4 The longest river in the world (6)

5 Bottom of a sea, river, or lake (3)

Shore Life

Across

2 Cold treat served in a cone (3,5)

5 Beach builder's creation (10)

8 Walk in shallow water; propel a canoe (6)

Down

1 Post-swim cloth used to dry your body (5)

3 Sideways-walking crustacean (4)

4 Shallow water where anemones and small fish can be found when the tide goes out (8)

6 Use a board to ride a wave (4)

7 The ebb and flow of the ocean; can be high or low (4)

Sports Club

Across

4 Sport played on an ice rink, with sticks and a puck (3,6)

6 Game played as an individual or pairs, with a shuttlecock (9)

7 Game of digs and spikes, sometimes played on a beach (10)

8 Team sport with scrums, played with an oblong ball (5)

Down

1 Football official; umpire (7)

2 Sport played by Serena Williams, Roger Federer, Rafael Nadal, and Emma Raducanu (6)

3 American game played with a bat and ball (8)

5 Extreme sport in which competitors scale very steep cliffs or walls (8)

All Things Pink

Across

3 A rosy hue (especially in the cheeks) (5)

6 Large fruit with striped green rind, pink flesh, and black seeds (10)

7 Stretchable pink chew (9)

Down

1 Fuzzy-skinned fruit with a pit (5)

2 Ballerina's skirt, often made of tulle (4)

3 Doll who's friends with Ken (6)

4 Fish with pink flesh (6)

5 Reef material; orangey-pink shade (5)

Museum Tour

Across

3 A painted picture of a person; not landscape (8)

5 A journey or route all the way around a particular place, such as an art gallery, sometimes led by a _ _ _ _ guide (4)

7 An online place filled with information about something, for example, about a museum (7)

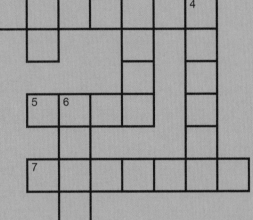

Down

1 A three-dimensional piece of art; Michelangelo's *David* or the bust of Nefertiti, for example (9)

2 Art show organizer; person responsible for a collection at a museum (7)

4 Entry permit; piece of paper or electronic code sometimes needed to gain entry to an exhibition (6)

6 Opposite of closed (4)

Space Invaders

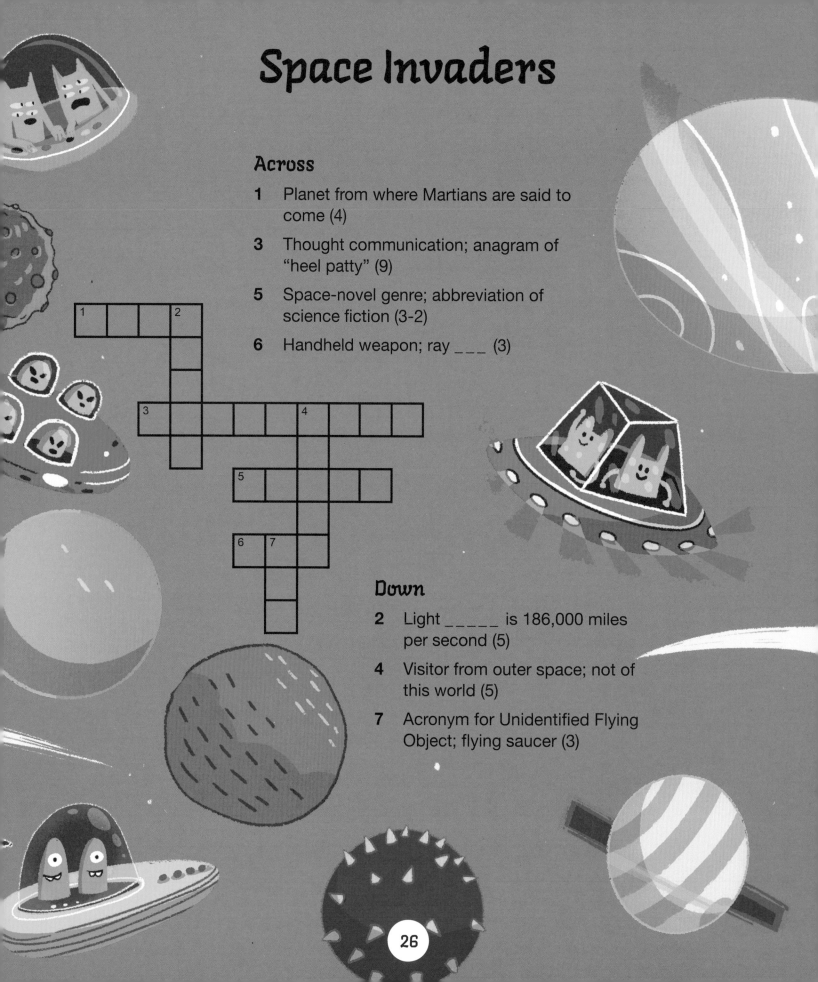

Across

1 Planet from where Martians are said to come (4)

3 Thought communication; anagram of "heel patty" (9)

5 Space-novel genre; abbreviation of science fiction (3-2)

6 Handheld weapon; ray ___ (3)

Down

2 Light _____ is 186,000 miles per second (5)

4 Visitor from outer space; not of this world (5)

7 Acronym for Unidentified Flying Object; flying saucer (3)

Medieval Manor

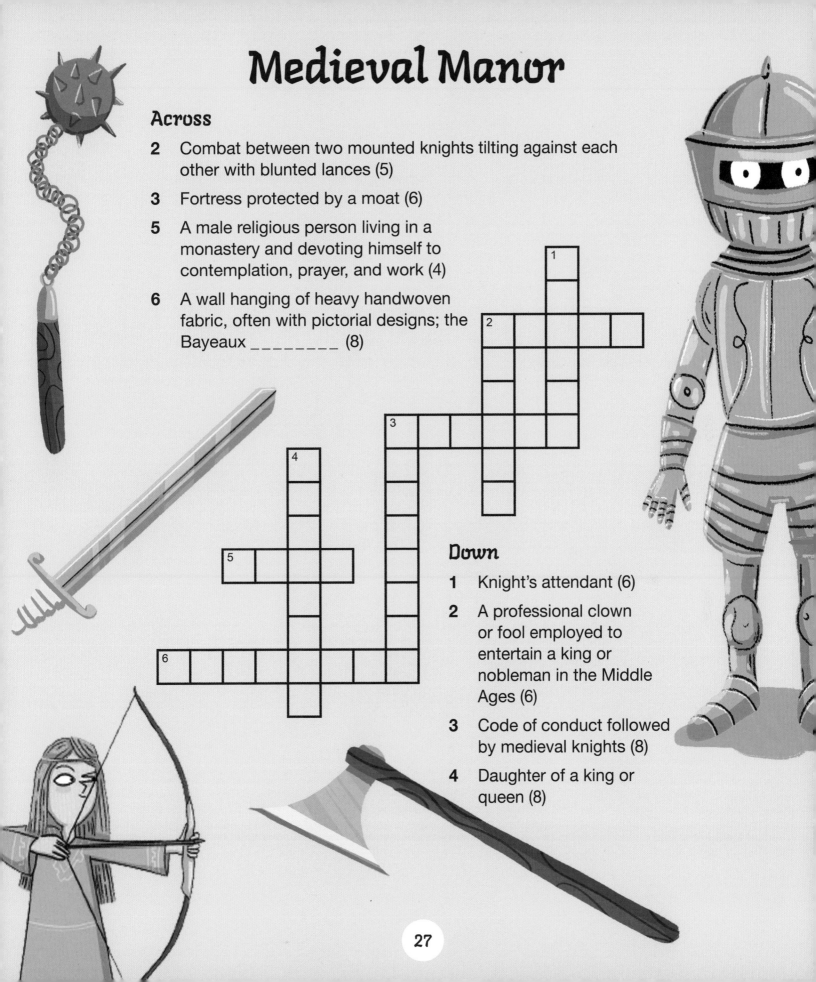

Across

2 Combat between two mounted knights tilting against each other with blunted lances (5)

3 Fortress protected by a moat (6)

5 A male religious person living in a monastery and devoting himself to contemplation, prayer, and work (4)

6 A wall hanging of heavy handwoven fabric, often with pictorial designs; the Bayeaux _ _ _ _ _ _ _ _ (8)

Down

1 Knight's attendant (6)

2 A professional clown or fool employed to entertain a king or nobleman in the Middle Ages (6)

3 Code of conduct followed by medieval knights (8)

4 Daughter of a king or queen (8)

Sweet Treats

Across

2 A cold treat, e.g., vanilla or chocolate (3,5)

5 Square or bar of very rich, squidgy chocolate cake, sometimes with nuts (7)

6 Small cake, usually baked in a paper case (6)

7 Unit of chocolate, gold, or soap (3)

8 A warm drink made with milk and sweetened cocoa (3,9)

Down

1 A French flaky pastry baked into a crescent shape (9)

3 A treat baked on a sheet, often including chocolate chips (6)

4 You can stir chocolate syrup into this to make chocolate ____ (4)

Dance Off!

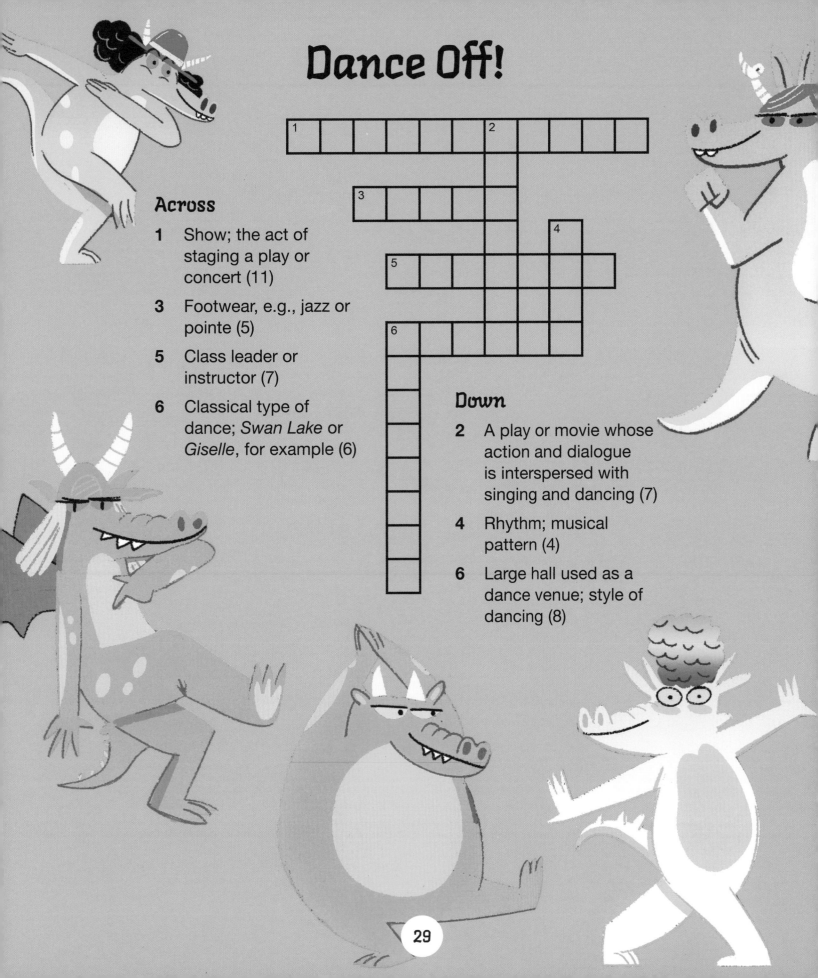

Across

1 Show; the act of staging a play or concert (11)

3 Footwear, e.g., jazz or pointe (5)

5 Class leader or instructor (7)

6 Classical type of dance; *Swan Lake* or *Giselle*, for example (6)

Down

2 A play or movie whose action and dialogue is interspersed with singing and dancing (7)

4 Rhythm; musical pattern (4)

6 Large hall used as a dance venue; style of dancing (8)

Awesome Aquarium

Across

2 Six-legged crustacean (4)

3 Tiny plant or animal organisms that drift in water; krill, for example (8)

4 Hard outer covering or case of certain organisms such as arthropods and turtles (5)

6 Eight-limbed sea creature (7)

7 Grit found on the ocean floor (4)

Down

1 Clownfish have black, white, and _ _ _ _ _ _ stripes (6)

2 Hard- or soft-shelled marine invertebrate (4)

4 Creature that squirts ink (5)

5 It forms reefs in warm seas (5)

Pizza Night

Across

3 Vegetable that might be sliced into rings and used as a topping (5)

4 Stretchy Italian cheese (10)

7 Italian sausage sliced very finely (9)

Down

1 Tropical fruit that some people like to put on pizza (9)

2 This red fruit can be made into ketchup or pizza sauce (6)

3 A kitchen appliance that can be used for baking (4)

5 Small green or black fruits with pits (6)

6 A mixture of flour, yeast, and water that is used to make a pizza base (5)

Shopping Spree

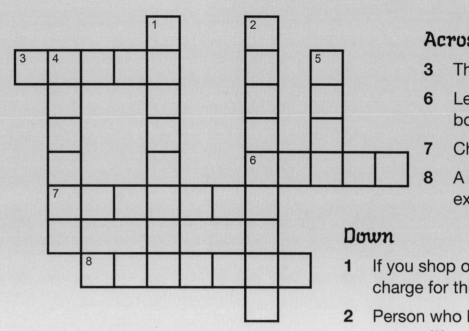

Across

3 The cost of an item for sale (5)

6 Ledge for holding stock; part of a bookcase (5)

7 Checkout printout (7)

8 A cashier takes this from a customer in exchange for goods (7)

Down

1 If you shop online, there might be a charge for this (8)

2 Person who helps customers find items in a store (9)

4 Take something back for a refund (6)

5 Discount; clearance event (4)

The World at Night

Across

2 This natural satellite of Earth is often visible in the night sky (4)

4 Medical place that is open all night (8)

5 Drivers can switch these on to illuminate their path after dark (10)

Down

1 Nocturnal dog-like mammal (3)

2 Twelve hours after noon; the witching hour (8)

3 Time before twilight (6)

6 The first light of day (4)

7 Snooze; get some shut-eye (5)

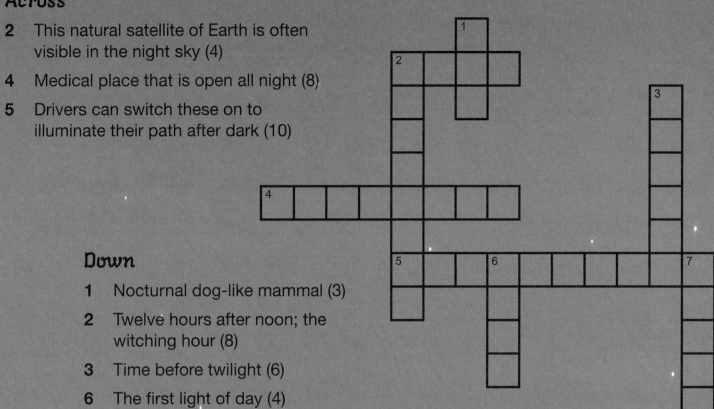

Plant Life

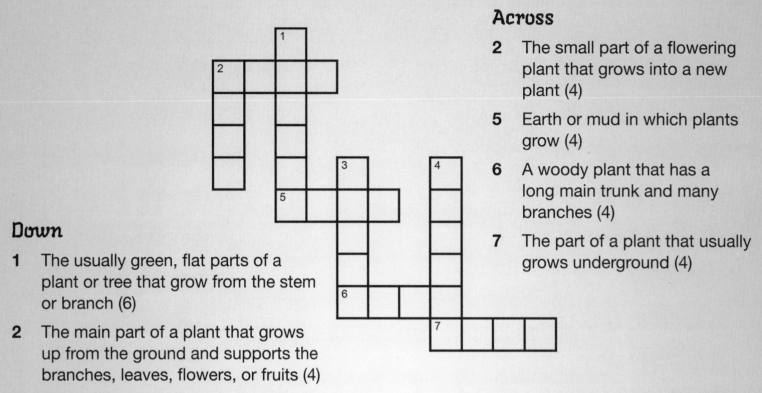

Across

2 The small part of a flowering plant that grows into a new plant (4)

5 Earth or mud in which plants grow (4)

6 A woody plant that has a long main trunk and many branches (4)

7 The part of a plant that usually grows underground (4)

Down

1 The usually green, flat parts of a plant or tree that grow from the stem or branch (6)

2 The main part of a plant that grows up from the ground and supports the branches, leaves, flowers, or fruits (4)

3 Energy emitted by the Sun; opposite of dark (5)

4 Blossom; the part of a plant that has petals (6)

At the Zoo

Across

1 Mammal with a very long neck (7)

3 Small South African mammal that lives in burrows and frequently stands on its hind legs (7)

7 Black-and-white seabird (7)

8 Slow-moving shelled reptile (8)

Down

2 Very large mammals with trunks (9)

4 Person whose job it is to look after animals at a zoo (6)

5 Ring-tailed primates from Madagascar (6)

6 King of the cats (4)

Lending Library

Across

2 Book filled with definitions of words (10)

3 Writer of a book, article, or document (6)

5 Receive as a loan (6)

6 Part of a website or a book (4)

7 Acquiring knowledge; discovering (8)

Down

1 A person who takes care of a collection of books (9)

3 Book of maps (5)

4 Work of fiction; new (5)

It's Electric!

Across

2 A thing sometimes made of rounded glass used to create electric light (4)

4 A machine that causes motion or power; part of a car (5)

5 Stop temporarily; button on remote (5)

7 Energy caused by the movement of electrons through matter; power (11)

Down

1 Degree of loudness; sound setting (6)

3 The closed path followed by an electric current; short _ _ _ _ _ _ _ (7)

6 A device that opens and closes an electrical circuit (6)

Fluttery Butterfly

Across

3 Most butterflies eat this sugary flower product (6)

5 Number of legs a butterfly has (3)

6 A butterfly's antennae and eyes are found on its _ _ _ _ (4)

7 Butterflies lay these, and they hatch into caterpillars (4)

8 Body parts used for flying (5)

Down

1 This species of butterfly migrates very long distances across Central and North America (7)

2 Pupa within its cocoon (9)

4 Butterflies usually lay their **7 down** on these plant parts (6)

38

Careers Fair

Across

2 An elected person who works in government (10)

4 A person who raises crops or animals (6)

6 This person treats sick or injured people (6)

7 A person who is responsible for enforcing the law (6,7)

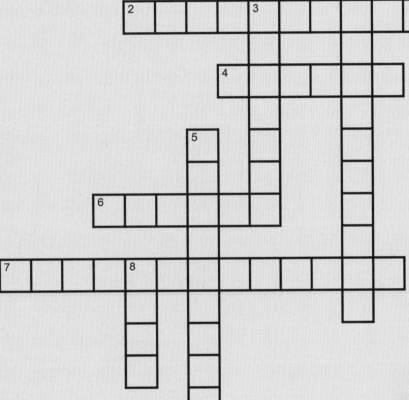

Down

1 Blaze battler; person who puts out flames (11)

3 Class leader; educator (7)

5 A person trained to travel in a spacecraft (9)

8 Someone in charge of a kitchen in a restaurant (4)

In the Desert

Across

3 Any of several species of four-legged reptiles (6)

5 Spiny succulent plant (6)

7 Animal with a hump or two (5)

8 Fennec _ _ _; small mammal with relatively large ears (3)

Down

1 Large Asian desert (4)

2 Very large North African desert (6)

4 Hills made of wind-blown sands (5)

6 Desert-dwelling arachnid with a sting in its tail (8)

40

Robot Reboot

Across

3 What a programmer writes (4)

5 A system of notation for writing computer programs, e.g., Python or Javascript (8)

7 Computer storage or capacity (6)

8 A device that detects and responds to changes in light, temperature, sound, or pressure, and then sends information to other instruments (6)

Down

1 AI stands for Artificial
_ _ _ _ _ _ _ _ _ _ _ _ (12)

2 Practical application of science (10)

4 TV channel changer (6)

6 A series of software instructions to a computer (7)

In the Garden

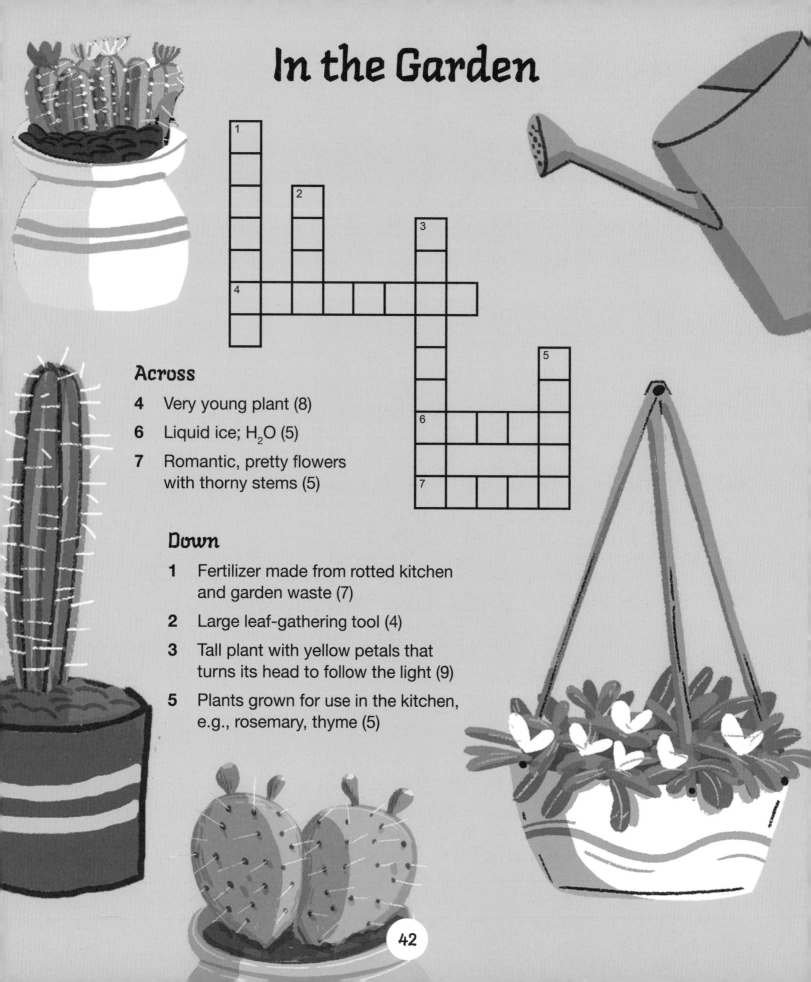

Across

4 Very young plant (8)

6 Liquid ice; H_2O (5)

7 Romantic, pretty flowers with thorny stems (5)

Down

1 Fertilizer made from rotted kitchen and garden waste (7)

2 Large leaf-gathering tool (4)

3 Tall plant with yellow petals that turns its head to follow the light (9)

5 Plants grown for use in the kitchen, e.g., rosemary, thyme (5)

Terrific Trees

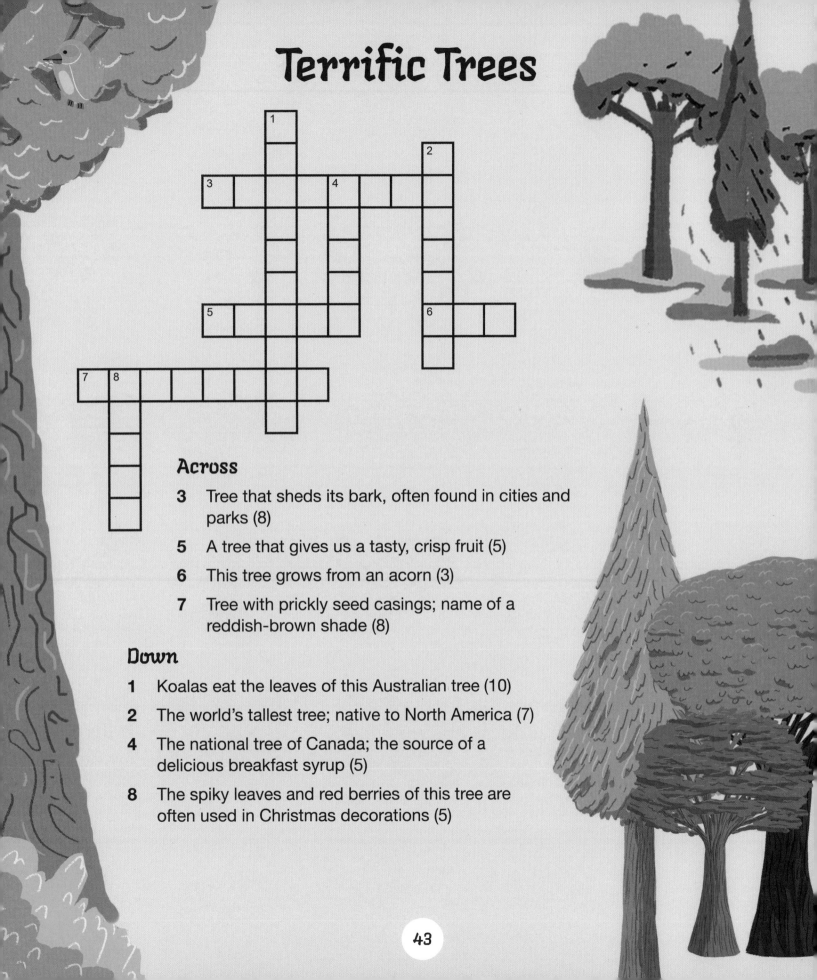

Across

3 Tree that sheds its bark, often found in cities and parks (8)

5 A tree that gives us a tasty, crisp fruit (5)

6 This tree grows from an acorn (3)

7 Tree with prickly seed casings; name of a reddish-brown shade (8)

Down

1 Koalas eat the leaves of this Australian tree (10)

2 The world's tallest tree; native to North America (7)

4 The national tree of Canada; the source of a delicious breakfast syrup (5)

8 The spiky leaves and red berries of this tree are often used in Christmas decorations (5)

At the Fair

Across

3 Electronic or paper permit to enter (6)

4 Tasty snack often sold at movies and fairs (7)

5 Spooky fairground ride (5,5)

7 A clairvoyant; crystal-ball reader (7,6)

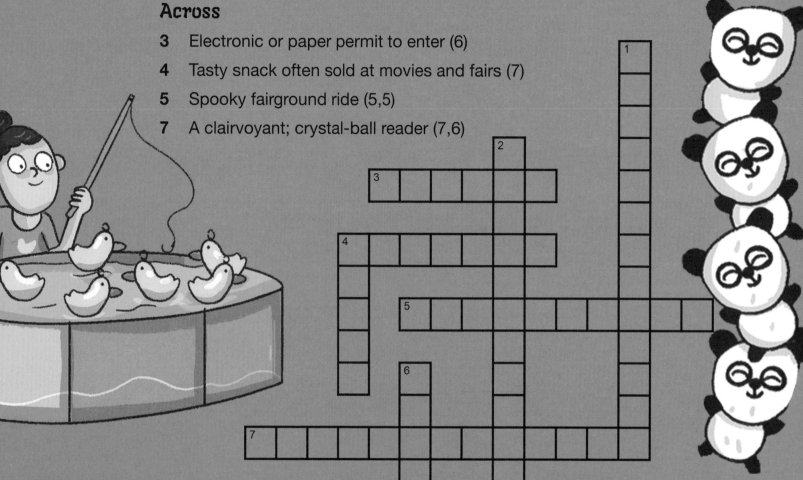

Down

1 Thrilling carnival ride (13)

2 Fairground attraction that goes around and around (6,5)

4 Objective for a fairground game player; something to be won (5)

6 Small horse, sometimes ridden at fairs (4)

Hiking Trip

Across

3 Device for finding direction (7)

5 Place for storytelling; marshmallow toaster (8)

6 Portable shelter (4)

8 Rucksack; bag carried on one's shoulders (8)

Down

1 You'll need a sturdy pair of these items of footwear on a long walk (5)

3 GPS display; navigator's need (3)

4 Roll-up bedding (8,3)

7 Top of a mountain or hill (4)

Exciting Egyptians

Across

1 Line of family rulers (7)

5 Ancient writing paper made from reeds (7)

7 Embalmed ancient Egyptian (5)

Down

2 The name of the longest river flowing through Egypt (4)

3 An Egyptian stone coffin (11)

4 An ancient Egyptian king (7)

6 Monumental Egyptian structure built as a tomb for an important person (7)

Build It Up

Across

1 Building blocks (6)

3 Person who works with water pipes (7)

5 Decorator; person who uses a brush on walls (7)

7 Protective headgear (4,3)

8 Top of a building (4)

Down

2 Person who works with wood (9)

4 Bond for **1 across**; weapon (6)

6 Item used to reach high places (6)

Big Blue Sky

Across

3 Filling a balloon with this can make it take off (3,3)

5 Insect similar to a butterfly (4)

7 Hovering insect with glasslike, iridescent wings (9)

Down

1 Thundery weather (5)

2 Thor's bolt; often accompanies thunder (9)

4 Egg-laying animal with two wings, two feet, and a body covered with feathers (4)

6 Fluffy sight in the sky; rain comes from this (5)

Treasure Trove

Across

2 A small band of metal or other hard material in the shape of a circle and worn on a finger (4)

4 Precious stone, usually red (4)

7 You might wear this decorative item around your throat (8)

8 A soft, heavy, yellow metal (4)

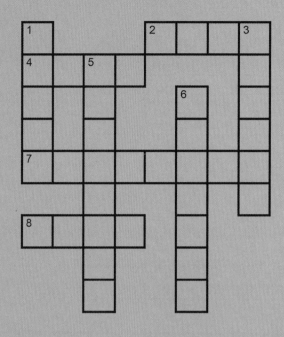

Down

1 A queen or king might wear one of these on the head (5)

3 A drinking vessel made of metal, sometimes decorated with patterns or jewels (6)

5 A band or chain worn around the wrist or arm as an ornament (8)

6 See-through, very hard precious stone (7)

Breakfast, Lunch, and Dinner

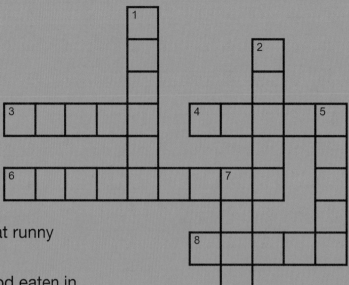

Across

3 Implement used to eat runny foods (5)

4 A small amount of food eaten in between regular meals (5)

6 Break in the middle of the school day (9)

8 A piece of furniture with a flat top supported by one or more legs (5)

Down

1 A very late breakfast, or a very early lunch (6)

2 Crockery; flat surface on which food can be served (5)

5 Tool used to cut food (5)

7 An occasion when food is prepared and eaten (4)

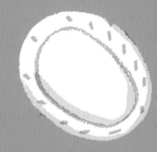
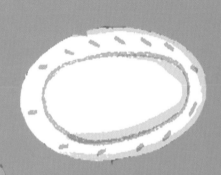

Puppy Party

Across

3 Large, spotted black-and-white breed of dog (9)

5 Small breed of dog named after a state in Mexico (9)

7 Dogs can be rewarded with these (6)

Down

1 A ball game for dogs (5)

2 The name of the nurse dog in *Peter Pan* (4)

4 A young dog (5)

5 A dog may wear this around its neck (6)

6 Sound heard at a dog park (4)

Viking Strike

Across

2 Norse god of thunder (4)

6 A surprise attack to steal valuable items and people (4)

7 A Viking home, comprised of one rectangular room (9)

8 To take over land (6)

Down

1 In Norse mythology, the hall for the souls of heroes (8)

3 Small stones bearing symbols; Viking letters of the alphabet (5)

4 Norse goddess of love (5)

5 Norse trickster god (4)

Fairy Dust

Across

3 A magical stick used to cast spells (4)

4 Things that fairies flap in order to fly (5)

7 Red-and-white fungus (9)

8 Mischievous sprite (5)

Down

1 Blooms; the part of a plant that has petals (7)

2 Chief fairy; head bee (5)

5 Sparkling decoration (7)

6 Bewitched; enchanted; spells (5)

On Safari

Across

2 A very large ape that lives in African forests (7)

4 A horse-like animal with a striped coat (5)

5 This African mammal has a cry that sounds like human laughter (5)

7 An enormous mammal with a very long nose called a trunk (8)

8 Big cat with a mane (4)

Down

1 An animal with a very long neck (7)

3 This big cat is the fastest animal on land (7)

6 An animal with horns, a long neck, long legs, and hooves (8)

Baking Day

Across

6 Crescent-shaped pastry (9)

7 Baked treat often wrapped in fluted paper cases (7)

8 A sweet substance in a crystal form (5)

Down

1 Chips, bars, syrup, mousse, cake, or ice cream can all be made with this (9)

2 A food made by baking a dough of flour or meal; can be sliced (5)

3 A solid white or yellow fat made by churning cream and used for cooking and spreading on bread (6)

4 Small, sweet, flat cakes baked from stiff dough (7)

5 The fine, ground meal or powder of wheat or other grain (5)

Superpowers

Across

2 Harry Potter's Cloak of _ _ _ _ _ _ _ _ _ _ _ _ (12)

4 Moving to the past or the future (4,6)

5 Way of getting through air, like Superman (6)

6 Moving by psychic power (13)

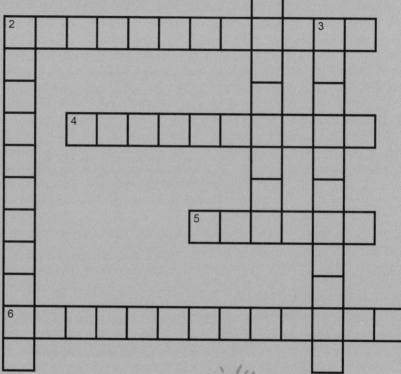

Down

1 Mind-to-mind communication (9)

2 The ability to live forever (11)

3 Power to move things by thinking (11)

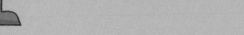

SOLUTIONS

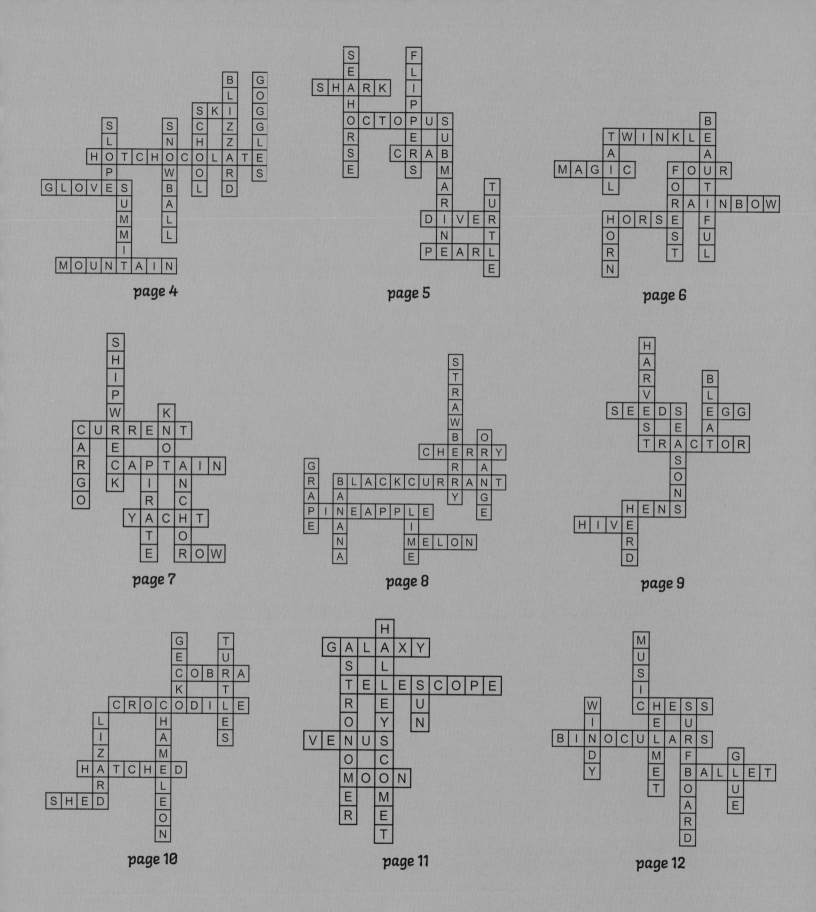

page 4

page 5

page 6

page 7

page 8

page 9

page 10

page 11

page 12

58

page 13

page 14

page 15

page 16

page 17

page 18

page 19

page 20

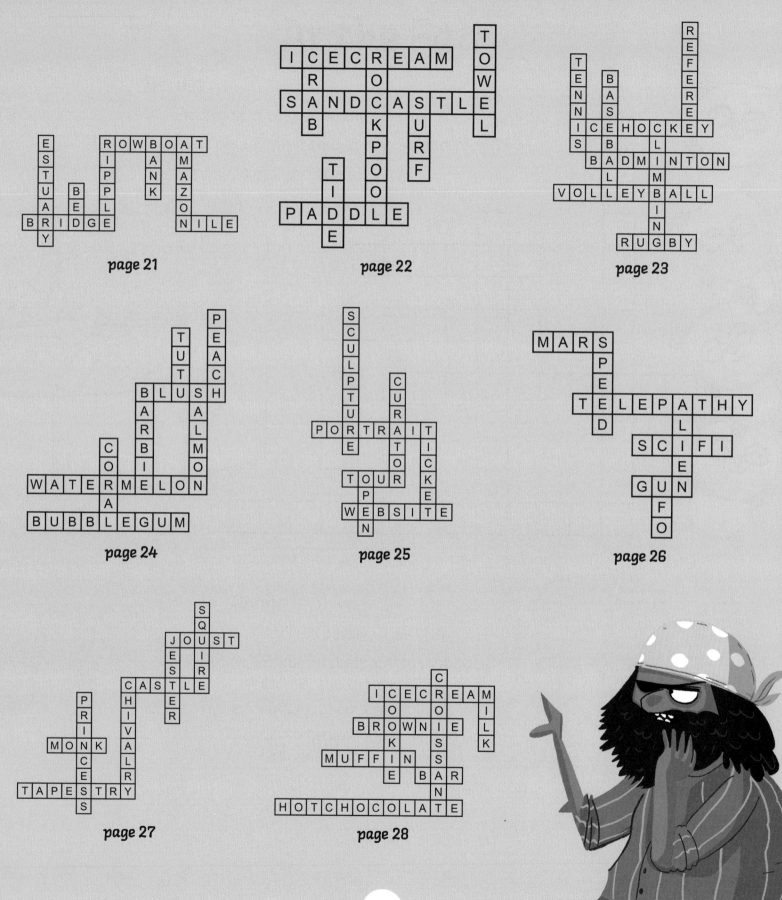

page 21

ESTUARY · ROWBOAT · RIPPLE · BANK · AMAZON · BEE · BRIDGE · NILE

page 22

ICECREAM · TOWEL · CRAB · ROCKPOOL · SANDCASTLE · SURF · TIDE · PADDLE

page 23

TENNIS · REFEREE · BASEBALL · ICEHOCKEY · BADMINTON · VOLLEYBALL · CLIMBING · RUGBY

page 24

PEACH · TUTU · BLUSH · BARBIE · ALMON · CORAL · WATERMELON · BUBBLEGUM

page 25

SCULPTURE · CURATOR · PORTRAIT · TICKET · TOUR · OPEN · WEBSITE

page 26

MARS · SPED · TELEPATHY · ALIEN · SCIFI · GUN · UFO

page 27

SQUIRE · JOUST · JESTER · CASTLE · CHIVALRY · PRINCESS · MONK · TAPESTRY

page 28

CROISSANT · ICECREAM · MILK · COOKIE · BROWNIE · MUFFIN · BAR · HOTCHOCOLATE

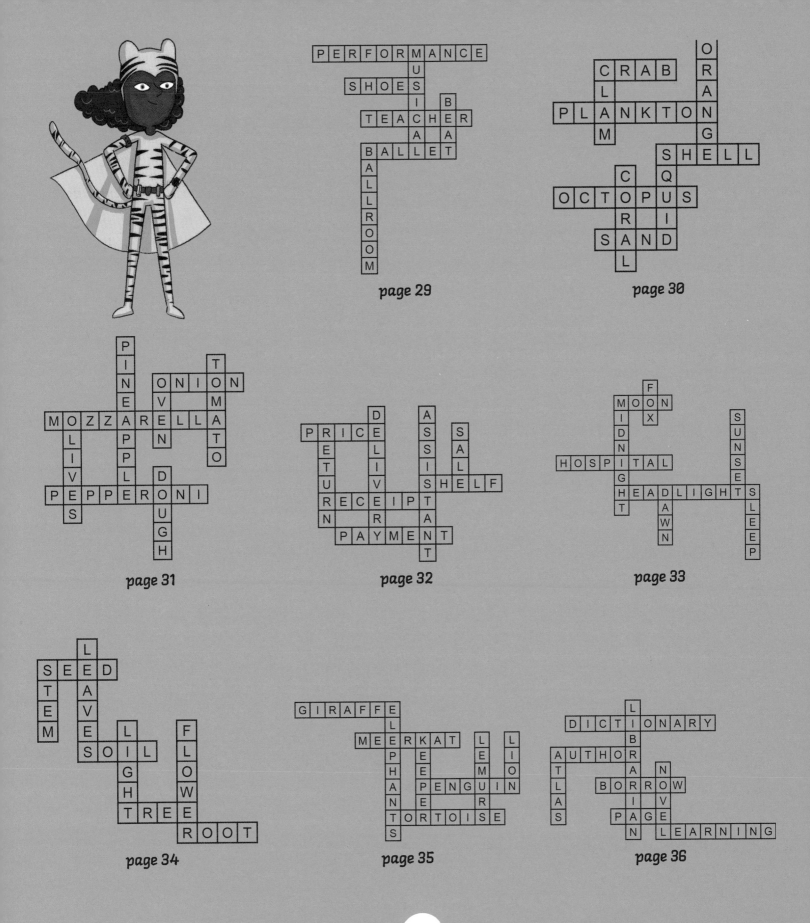

page 29

page 30

page 31

page 32

page 33

page 34

page 35

page 36

page 37

VOLUME, BULB, MOTOR, CIRCUIT, PAUSE, SWITCH, ELECTRICITY

page 38

MONARCH, NECTAR, CHRYSALIS, LEAVES, SIX, HEAD, EGGS, WINGS

page 39

POLITICIAN, FIREFIGHTER, TEACHER, FARMER, ASTRONAUT, DOCTOR, POLICE OFFICER, CHEF

page 40

GOB, SAHARA, LIZARD, DUNES, CACTUS, CAMEL, SCORPION, FOX

page 41

TECHNOLOGY, INTELLIGENCE, CODE, LANGUAGE, REMOTE, MEMORY, PROGRAM, SENSOR

page 42

COMPOST, RAKE, SEEDLING, SUNFLOWER, WATER, HERB, ROSES

page 43

EUCALYPTUS, SYCAMORE, REDWOOD, MAPLE, APPLE, OAK, CHESTNUT, HOLLY

page 44

ROLLERCOASTER, TICKET, FERRIS WHEEL, POPCORN, GHOST TRAIN, PRIZE, PONY, FORTUNE TELLER

62

page 45

page 46

page 47

page 48

page 49

page 50

page 51

page 52

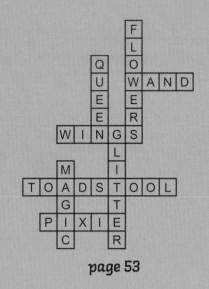

page 53

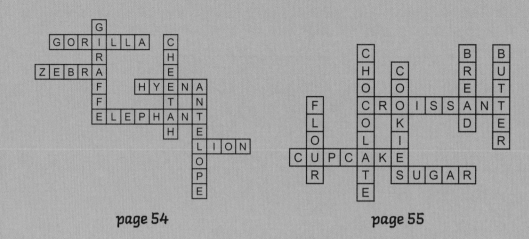

page 54

Page 55 crossword:

page 55

page 56